Great Explorers

Exploring the Pacific

The Expeditions of James Cook

Andrew Langley

Illustrated by David McAllister

Chelsea Juniors
A division of Chelsea House Publishers

Great Explorers
Discovering the New World
Exploring the Pacific
The Great Polar Adventure
Journey into Space

This edition published by Chelsea House Publishers, a
division of Main Line Book Co., 300 Park Avenue South,
New York, New York 10010, by arrangement with
Irwin Jorvik Ltd.

1 3 5 7 9 8 6 4 2

ISBN 0-7910-2819-4

Contents

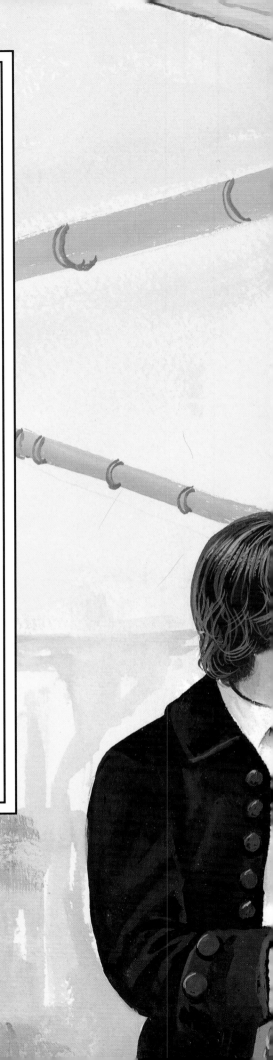

Going to Sea

Imagine yourself onboard a small sailing ship two hundred years ago, sailing through the perilous southern seas. The ship's ropes and mast are heavy with ice, and the sails are frozen solid, yet with bare hands and bare feet the crew must man the ship. You have already been at sea for 18 months and it will be another 18 months before you return to your home. But you go on because you are sailing with James Cook, one of the greatest seamen of his day, and you are searching for the great Southern Continent.

James Cook had always wanted to be a sailor but his father discouraged him. He was born in Yorkshire, England, in 1728. Drawn to the sea, he went at 17 to work in a grocery shop in the coastal fishing village of Staithes. But shopkeeping was much too dull for Cook, and a year later he persuaded his father to let him go to sea.

Cook began his seafaring career as a deckhand on a collier, a little ship that carried coal down to London. In his spare time, he studied hard, learning the skills that would make him a ship's captain. After ten years, his employer offered to put him in command of a ship, but, to everyone's astonishment, Cook refused. Instead, he joined the Royal Navy as an ordinary sailor.

Determined to be a success, Cook learned quickly and performed every task skillfully and well. Soon, he rose to the rank of master and, in 1758, he was put in command of a warship.

DID YOU KNOW?

The **British Royal Navy** was not exactly a great place to work in the eighteenth century. Navy ships were often filthy, and their food and water were disgusting. More sailors died from disease than in battle!

The Unknown Continent

The Pacific Ocean, where Cook made most of his voyages, was still a huge mystery in the 1760s. Many sailors had crossed it, but no one had explored it all. There were many questions to answer. How big was this great ocean? How many islands were there?

The biggest puzzle of all was the "Southern Continent." People knew all about the continents of Europe, Asia and Africa. They had explored the two new ones – North America and South America. Many believed there could be yet another rich, new continent at the southern end of the world.

Where was this unknown land? The Pacific seemed to go on forever. Explorers had found the coasts of Australia and New Zealand, but these were not extensive enough to be the shores of the great, undiscovered continent. Others had seen what appeared to be a distant land in the far south, but had not dared to explore it.

The southern seas were dangerous. Sailors had to battle with sudden fogs and typhoons, as well as swirling currents. It was also very cold, with violent snowstorms, and ice clung to the sails.

In 1768, the British government decided to send an expedition in search of the Southern Continent. They wanted to be the first to find it. There might be gold there, or some other kind of treasure. If the unknown land belonged to the British, it might make them even more rich and powerful.

DID YOU KNOW?

This is what people thought the world looked like around the time of Cook.

DID YOU KNOW?

Typhoons, or hurricanes, are the most violent storms known. They are most frequent in tropical regions, especially in the warm seas of the western Atlantic, Pacific, and Indian Oceans. Typhoons can be as big as 372 miles (600 km) across with walls of cloud 9 miles (15 km) high and winds of up to 99 mph (160 km/h). Typhoon Tip of 1979 was more than 136 miles (2,200 km) across with winds of 186 mph (300 km/h)!

To the Pacific

By this time, James Cook had become an outstanding sailor. He had spent five years making maps of the coast of Newfoundland in North America. France and Britain were at war in the area and it was difficult and dangerous work, but he had done it very well. He also carried on with his studies, learning more mathematics and astronomy.

Cook was the ideal person to lead the expedition to find the Southern Continent. The navy promoted him to lieutenant, and gave him command of the ship *Endeavour*. It had a crew of 94, and enough stores to last for more than a year.

The *Endeavour* sailed from Plymouth on August 6, 1768. Onboard was Joseph Banks, a noted naturalist, with several assistants and artists. The ship stopped at Madeira to take on extra wine. Then Cook sailed safely across the Atlantic, around Cape Horn, at the southern tip of South America, and into the mysterious Pacific Ocean.

First the expedition sailed to the island of Tahiti to build an observatory. From there, scientists could watch the planet Venus as it passed in front of the Sun. This was called the Transit of Venus. It happened very rarely. By watching it carefully, the scientists could find out the distance between the Earth and the Sun.

DID YOU KNOW?

Tahiti is part of the Polynesian Group of islands. These islands are often described as a "tropical paradise" because they are always warm and humid, with plenty of rain to keep them lush and green. They are also very beautiful. Coconut palms and guava trees grow wild and the islands are covered with sweet-smelling flowers of many colors.

DID YOU KNOW?

Transits of Venus occur roughly every 100 years, in pairs, eight years apart. They only happen in June and December. To use the transit to find the distance between the Earth and the Sun, scientists had to observe the transit from different places on the Earth. That is why they went to Tahiti. The next pair of transits will take place on June 8, 2004, and June 6, 2012.

On Board the *Endeavour*

Cook must have felt at home on the *Endeavour*. It was a collier, just like the ships he had sailed on when he first went to sea. It was a small vessel, only 105 feet (32 m) long, and less than 30 feet (9 m) wide, with three masts and six guns. Her bottom was flat and shallow. It was covered with extra wood and flat-headed nails hammered in close together. These kept out the tiny ship worms which might damage the hull.

The *Endeavour* was not fast or pretty, but she was very strong and well made. There was plenty of room for stores and equipment. There was even space for a goat, which gave fresh milk.

Cook was determined that his crew should be healthy. He ordered each man to have a cold bath every day. He made sure their bedding was aired and their sleeping quarters cleaned. They also had much healthier food than other sailors of the time. Whenever possible, they ate fresh meat and caught their own fresh fish. The water barrels were scrubbed out regularly.

Above all, Cook wanted to prevent scurvy. This was a disease that killed many sailors. Cook made the crew eat fruit and pickled vegetables. They didn't like this food, but they ate it, and during the voyage not one person on the *Endeavour* died from scurvy.

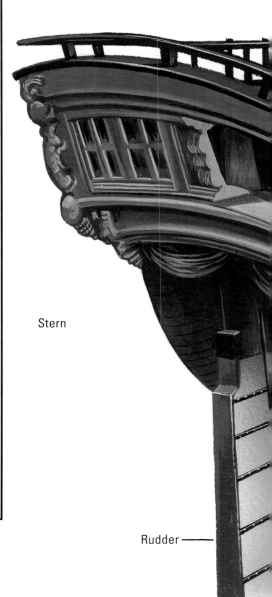

This is what a ship of Columbus's time would look like if you could see inside it.

Stern

Rudder ——

DID YOU KNOW?

Scurvy is a disease caused by not having enough Vitamin C in your diet. Victims suffer from swollen and bleeding gums, loosened teeth, and stiffness in the joints and may die. It can be cured by eating lemons, limes, or oranges, which contain lots of Vitamin C.

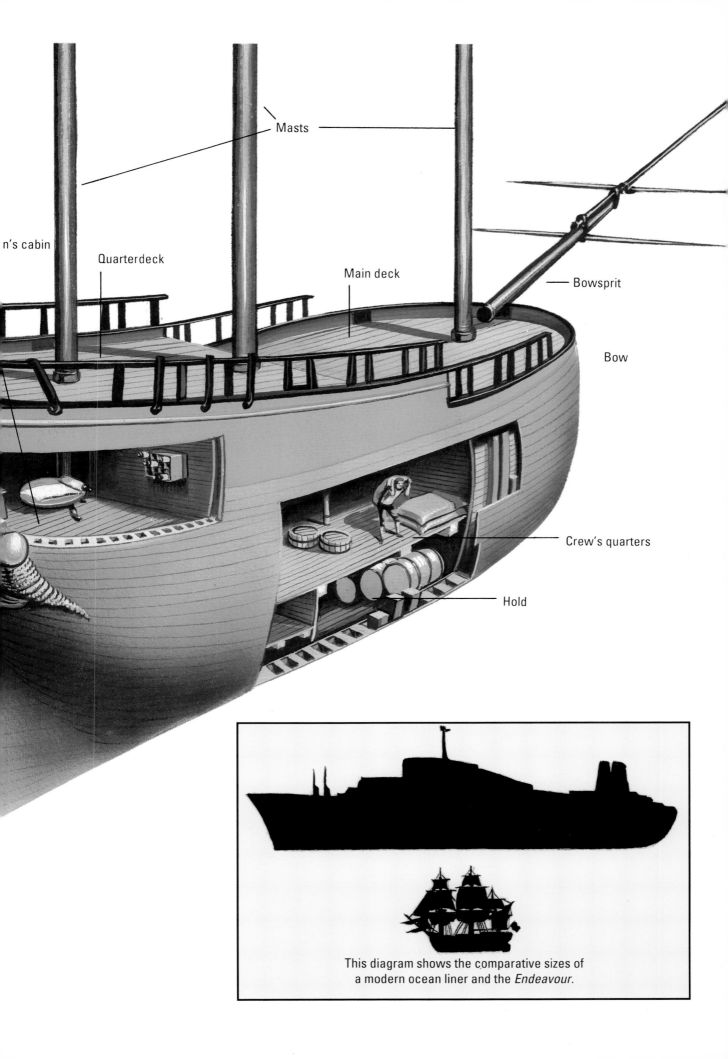

Masts

n's cabin

Quarterdeck

Main deck

Bowsprit

Bow

Crew's quarters

Hold

This diagram shows the comparative sizes of a modern ocean liner and the *Endeavour*.

Paradise Island

The *Endeavour* dropped anchor at Tahiti on April 13, 1769. The native people on the island greeted them joyously. The place seemed like a paradise, full of beauty and happiness. There was plenty to eat, and the people were generous. But the Tahitians felt entitled to take as well as give. They took nails and muskets and snuffboxes and a telescope. One even managed to take Cook's stockings from under his pillow – while he was lying on them!

Cook set about his first task. The observatory was soon built. On the day of the Transit of Venus, the scientists watched and made their measurements. Meanwhile, Banks was busy collecting flowers and insects.

By July the work was complete. The ship sailed southward. But there was no sign of an unknown continent. Storms forced the *Endeavour* to turn westward instead. Finally, they sighted land. Was this the great continent they were searching for? It turned out to be New Zealand. Some of the native Maoris were not as friendly as the Tahitians, but Cook and his men did venture ashore for water and fresh food. In doing so, they became the first Europeans ever to set foot there.

Then Cook made a voyage around New Zealand's coastline. As he went, he charted the shores. In this way, he proved that New Zealand was composed of two separate islands. It was not connected to a huge southern continent.

Polynesian peoples are tall with light brown skin and black hair. They often live in large families with children, parents, sisters, aunts, uncles, nephews, nieces, and grandparents all together. Children are expected to help out around the house when they can, but they are usually left to play their favorite games. These include wrestling, dart-throwing, juggling, singing, and dancing.

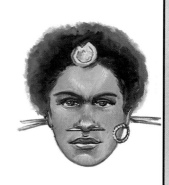

The Great Reef

It had been a long and difficult voyage. Their mission was over and they could now go straight home. But Cook wanted to carry on exploring. He talked to his men, and they agreed to look for the east coast of Australia. Dutch explorers had sailed past Australia a hundred years before. They had seen Tasmania and the wild west coast. But no Europeans had so far set foot on the east coast.

The *Endeavour* soon reached the southeast tip of Australia. Then Cook turned north. They landed at a place Cook called Botany Bay. They were attacked by Aborigines, but the scientists were also thrilled to see a new kind of animal — a kangaroo.

Further north, the ship entered the Great Barrier Reef. This was a perilous place, with huge teeth of jagged coral hidden beneath the waves. One night there was a crash. The *Endeavour* had hit the coral. She was stuck fast, and water was pouring in. Cook ordered the men to throw guns and stores overboard, until at last the tide lifted the ship off the reef.

After repairing the hole, Cook found his way out of the terrible coral. He headed for home, but soon real tragedy struck. The *Endeavour* stopped at Batavia, in Java, where many of the crew caught deadly diseases. Only seven men had been lost during the long voyage, but 33 more died in Batavia.

DID YOU KNOW?

Abel Janszoon Tasman was one of the greatest of the Dutch navigators and explorers. He was born around 1603 and made his two greatest voyages between 1642 and 1644, exploring the Indian Ocean, Australasia, and the South Pacific Ocean. He was the first European to see Tasmania, New Zealand, Tonga, and Fiji.

DID YOU KNOW?

The **Great Barrier Reef** is made of the skeletons of millions upon millions of tiny animals called coral polyps. These stick together to form colonies. The Great Barrier Reef is the largest structure ever built by living creatures. It is so large that it can be seen from the Moon. It is over 1,240 miles (2,000 km) long, covers an area of 79,993 square miles (207,000 sq km) and contains over 350 different species of coral, anemones, worms, lobsters, crayfish, prawns, crabs, and a huge and colorful variety of fish and birds.

Into the Ice

Cook arrived back at Plymouth in July 1771, but he did not stay in England for long. Exactly a year later he set out again from the same port. This time he had two ships, the *Resolution* and the *Adventure*. Both were sturdy colliers, just like the *Endeavour*.

Cook was now a commander. Once again, his task was to look for the Southern Continent, and he planned to explore the whole of the South Pacific in his search.

The two ships reached the Cape of Good Hope, on the tip of southern Africa, then they headed due south. The air grew colder, and the crew saw icebergs for the first time. A few weeks later, the *Resolution* and *Adventure* crossed the Antarctic Circle. They were the first European ships to go so far south. There it was even colder. The sailors' bare hands froze to the rigging, gales shrieked about them, and the shifting ice groaned and thundered.

In the end Cook could go no farther. He turned back to New Zealand, where they spent the winter months. They repaired the ships and took on fresh food. It was time for the second part of the search. The expedition went eastward, landing at Tahiti and Tonga, but during a storm the two ships lost sight of each other. The captain of the *Adventure* gave up and sailed back to England, leaving Cook's *Resolution* all alone.

DID YOU KNOW?

Icebergs are huge lumps of ice that have broken off from ice sheets and drift around in the sea. The largest icebergs break off from the edge of Antarctica. Icebergs are always a hazard to shipping. Nowadays they are sometimes towed by powerful tugs away from shipping lanes.

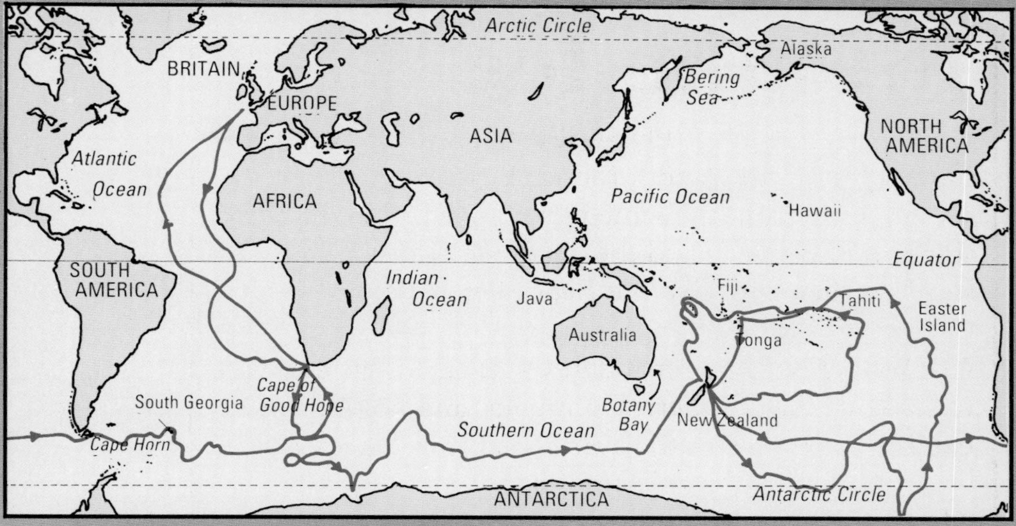
Arctic Circle
Alaska
BRITAIN
EUROPE
Bering Sea
ASIA
NORTH AMERICA
Atlantic Ocean
AFRICA
Pacific Ocean
Hawaii
SOUTH AMERICA
Equator
Indian Ocean
Java
Fiji
Tahiti
Easter Island
Australia
Tonga
Cape of Good Hope
South Georgia
Botany Bay
New Zealand
Southern Ocean
Cape Horn
ANTARCTICA
Antarctic Circle

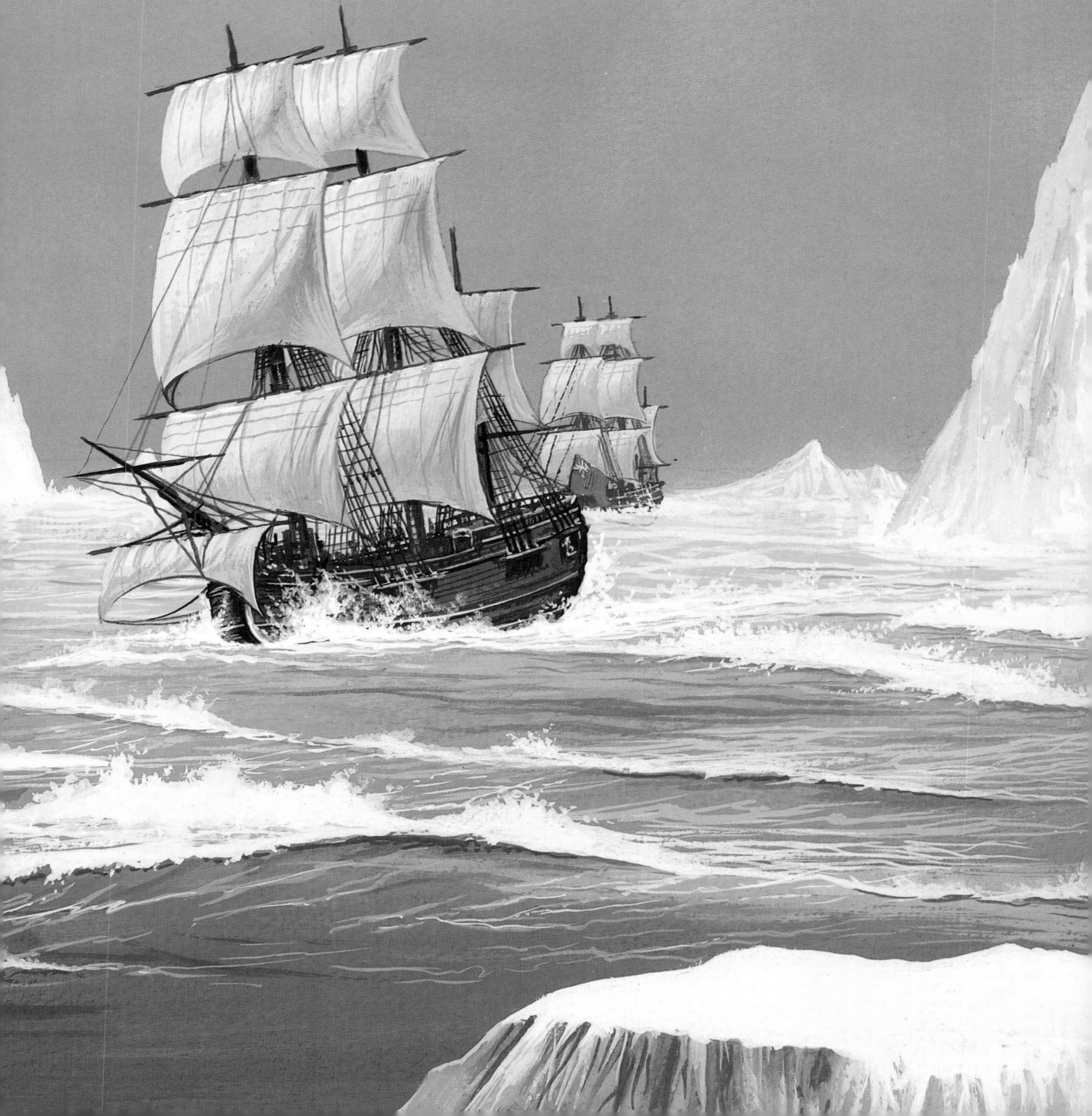

Around the World

At the end of 1773, Cook headed south on the third leg of his great voyage. The *Resolution* zigzagged across the last unexplored part of the South Pacific. Soon, she was inside the Antarctic Circle again.

Each day the weather became worse. The waves were huge and fog swirled around. High winds brought blizzards of snow and sleet. Worst of all was the ice. The sails and ropes froze as hard as steel. All around were jagged icebergs and sheets of pack ice. Somehow, Cook managed to steer his way between all these obstacles.

In the end he was brought to a halt. There in front of the ship stretched a wall of solid ice as high as a mountain. They had reached farther south than anyone had ever done before. If the Southern Continent existed, it was too inhospitable to be explored or exploited.

It was time to go home. Cook was exhausted and very ill. The *Resolution* returned to Tahiti, visiting Easter Island on the way. Early in 1775 Cook rounded Cape Horn and explored the island of South Georgia.

When Cook reached England, he had completed an amazing journey. He had traveled over 117,800 miles (190,000 km), and had gone around the world. He had proved that there was no great lush continent in the South.

DID YOU KNOW?

Easter Island lies in the Pacific some 2,232 miles (3,600 km) west of Chile. It is best known for its massive stone statues that have been carved from soft volcanic rock. The stones are formed into giant figures between 10 and 39 feet in height and weighing up to 45 tons. They were probably made around A.D. 1000-1600, but, to this day, no one really knows why.

DID YOU KNOW?

The **aurora australis** was seen by Cook on his voyage in Antarctic waters in 1773. These strange lights in the sky can be white or colored red, green, yellow, or blue. Sometimes they look like rays from a searchlight, at other times they can look like darting flames or billowing curtains.

The Way to the North

Cook had solved one great mystery. Now the British Navy asked him to solve another. Was there a northwest passage?

For centuries, sailors had searched for a sea route to the north of the American continent. This would link the Atlantic and Pacific oceans so that sailing ships would no longer have to negotiate the dangerous Cape Horn at the tip of South America. But the northern route, if it existed, seemed to be blocked by ice and hundreds of islands.

On July 11, 1776, Cook set out once again in the *Resolution*. Her sister ship was yet another collier, the *Discovery*. On board were some sheep and cattle – presents for the Pacific islanders.

It was soon clear that the *Resolution* was in a bad state. Her hull leaked, and one of the masts was cracked. During the long voyage she often had to be repaired. In spite of this, both ships sailed safely to New Zealand and Tahiti. Then they carried on toward the northern Pacific, where few Europeans had ever been before.

Early in 1778, Cook made his last great discovery. He sighted a group of islands. They were surrounded by cliffs that were pounded by huge rolling waves. This island group is known today as Hawaii.

The Hawaiians were very friendly. In fact, they seemed to think that Cook was a god. They bowed before him and gave him gifts. No one suspected the tragedy that was to strike exactly a year later.

DID YOU KNOW?

The **Hawaiian Islands,** and many other islands in the Pacific, are actually formed on the tops of volcanoes that go right down to the seabed. One of the islands in the Hawaiian group sits on top of a mountain that rises 30,020 feet (9,150 m) above the ocean floor. That's even higher than Mt. Everest.

The Fatal Return

The *Resolution* and the *Discovery* left Hawaii on their quest for the Northwest Passage. They followed the coastline of America, battling against fierce gales. The coast seemed endless, but at last they rounded the Alaska Peninsula. The expedition had now reached the Bering Sea, a small stretch of ocean between North America and Asia.

Cook passed through the Bering Strait, where the two continents are only about 50 miles (80 km) apart. Only a few days later, he saw a familiar sight — ice. His path was blocked by the Arctic pack ice. There seemed to be no passage to the Atlantic here.

So Cook turned back to Hawaii. Once again, he was welcomed as a god, with banquets and presents. The islanders lavished much of their precious wealth and food on the visitors, but they couldn't understand why Cook, the "god," had no gifts for them, especially the iron that they valued highly. They must have been glad to see Cook's men sail away in February 1779, and angry to see the ships return a few days later. The *Resolution* needed another new mast!

This time there was no welcome, and the Hawaiians began to take from the ships what they felt they should have been given. Cook lost his temper and went ashore with armed men to recover the goods. Fighting broke out, and he was hacked to the ground and killed.

DID YOU KNOW?

Walruses were probably among the strangest creatures that Cook saw during his explorations. They are heavy-bodied animals, up to 12 feet (3.7 m) in length and weighing up to $2^1/2$ tons (1,260 kg). They have huge tusks (which are actually long canine teeth). These may be as long as 3 feet (1 m) and can weigh 12 pounds (5.4 kg).

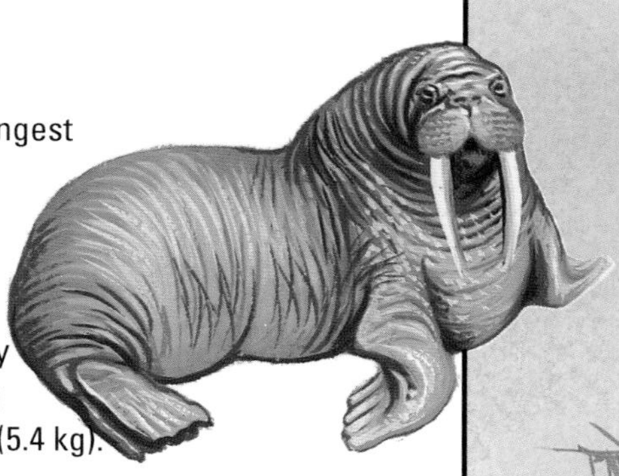

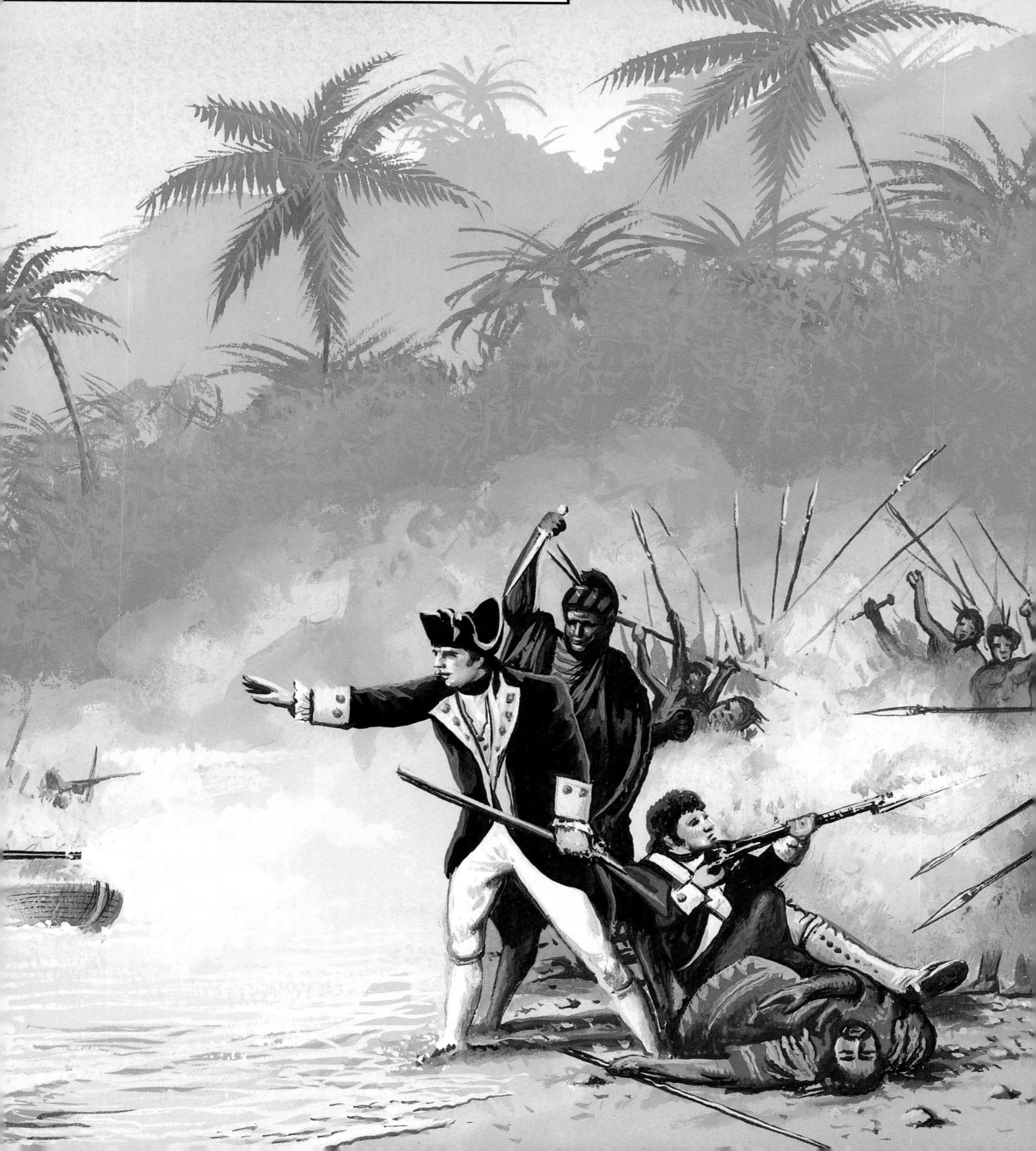

The Legacy of Cook

Cook was a brave and determined man and a great navigator and explorer. He opened up the Pacific Ocean to later explorers and scientists by accurately and painstakingly mapping its coastline and islands. He is also the father of Antarctic exploration. He was one of the first long-distance explorers to make use of the chronometer, a very accurate timepiece that made precise navigation possible.

He pioneered the better treatment of ships' crews through his insistence on fresh meat, fruit, and vegetables in every seaman's diet. In doing so, he helped rid the seafaring world of the scourge of scurvy.

He tried to behave honorably toward the native people he met and was very distressed by the devastating effect that European diseases had on their numbers. Sadly, this attitude died with him and the legacy of Cook's voyages for the Pacific populations was largely one of misery and death.

Cook had claimed Australia as a British possession. The British government decided to use it as a penal colony. The first convicts and their guards landed at Botany Bay in 1788. As more convicts and free settlers arrived, the native Aborigines were forced to retreat from their ancient lands. They were helpless against European guns. Many also died from European diseases. On Tasmania, every single Aborigine was murdered or shipped away.

It was the same story in New Zealand. By 1840, half the native Maori people had been wiped out by warfare and disease.

DID YOU KNOW?

The **diseases** that killed many Pacific islanders included measles and smallpox. These were common in Europe where people had been exposed to the diseases for so long that many were immune, or could not catch them. But they could carry the diseases. When the islanders caught the disease, they had no immunity and died in the thousands.

Transportation was used as a means of punishment in eighteenth-century Britain because the prisons were so overcrowded. In those days, people could be imprisoned for even the smallest crimes, like stealing a loaf of bread to feed their children. Transportation meant that they were sent away from their families, perhaps forever.

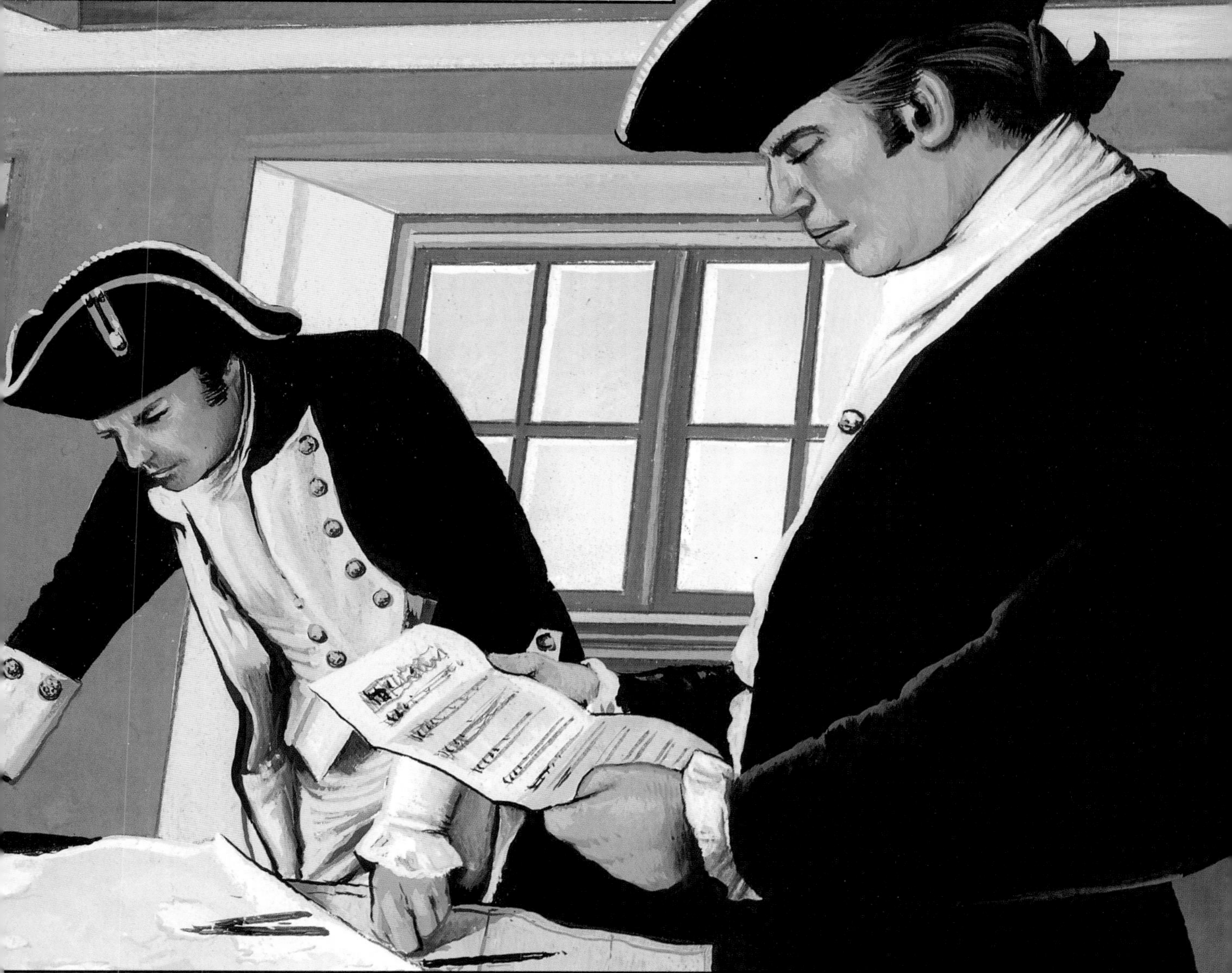

DID YOU KNOW?

The **chronometer** that Cook took with him on his second voyage, was the first ship's timepiece that was accurate enough to keep time with any degree of accuracy. It enabled Cook to pinpoint exactly his ship's east-west position.

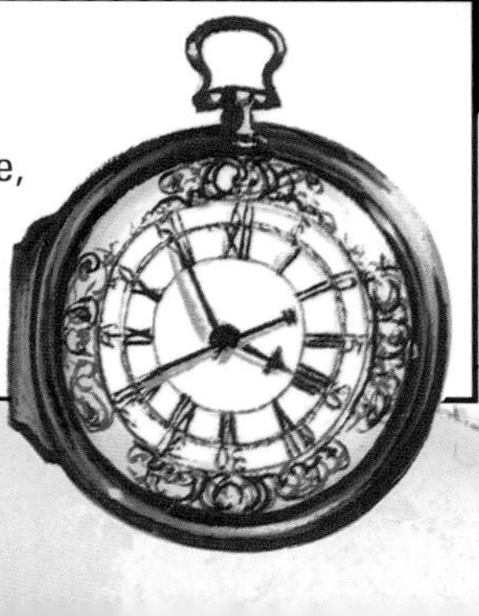

The Pacific Today

A hundred years after Cook's death, much of the culture of the Pacific island peoples had been destroyed by Europeans in search of riches from trading or growing crops. Yet today, some still survives. Most islanders still live in small farming or fishing villages. They have the same kinds of houses, clothes, and food as their ancestors. They speak the same languages and some follow the old religions.

The islanders now face new invaders — tourists. They bring money, but they also bring the need for hotels, roads, shops, and airports. Many fear that tourism will damage the traditional life on the islands.

The way of life of the Australian Aborigines is under much greater threat. At first they lost their land to farmers who brought cattle and sheep to graze on the wide grasslands. Now, more land is being destroyed so that valuable minerals such as gold, iron, and uranium can be extracted. Today, the Aborigines have lost nearly all their territory and many live in towns.

Another threat to the Pacific is pollution. Scientists have found that waste products such as sewage and spilled oil are destroying the ocean's wildlife. Parts of the Pacific are also being used to test nuclear weapons. The future for this mighty ocean that Cook loved so much is far from secure.

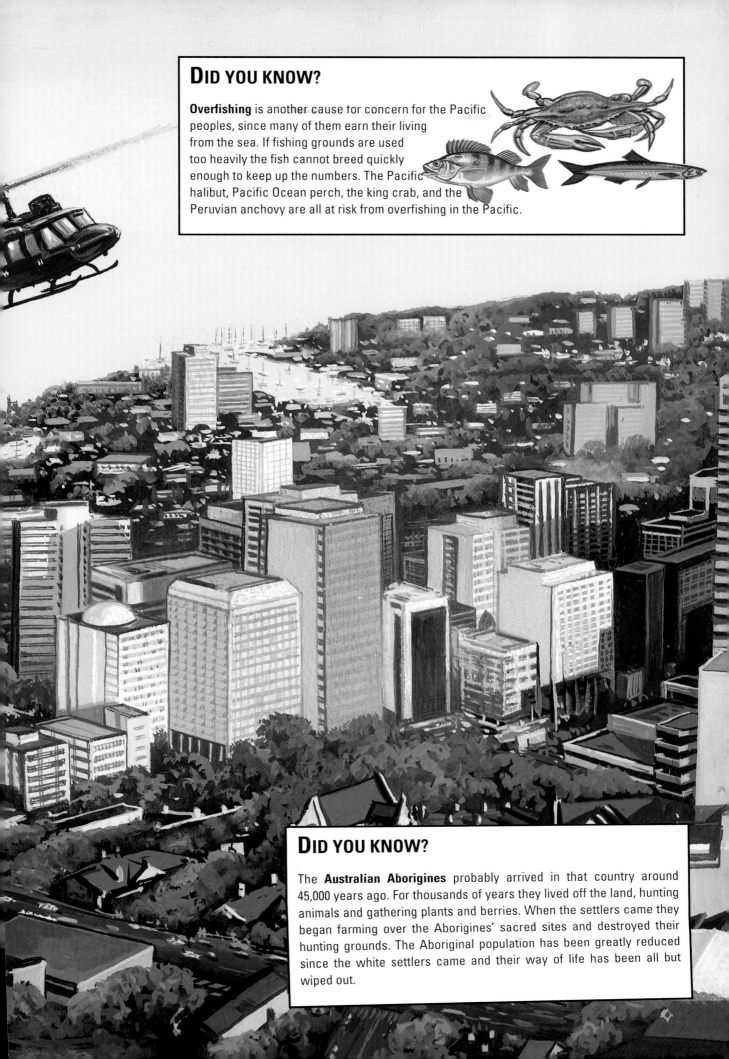

DID YOU KNOW?

Overfishing is another cause for concern for the Pacific peoples, since many of them earn their living from the sea. If fishing grounds are used too heavily the fish cannot breed quickly enough to keep up the numbers. The Pacific halibut, Pacific Ocean perch, the king crab, and the Peruvian anchovy are all at risk from overfishing in the Pacific.

DID YOU KNOW?

The **Australian Aborigines** probably arrived in that country around 45,000 years ago. For thousands of years they lived off the land, hunting animals and gathering plants and berries. When the settlers came they began farming over the Aborigines' sacred sites and destroyed their hunting grounds. The Aboriginal population has been greatly reduced since the white settlers came and their way of life has been all but wiped out.

Glossary

Antarctic Circle An imaginary circle, drawn around the Earth, marking off the southern polar region from the warmer seas to the north.

Astronomy The study of the stars, planets, and space.

Blizzard A severe snowstorm.

Missionaries People who travel to a different place or country to tell people about their religion.

Naturalist Someone who studies plants and animals.

Observatory A place with telescopes and other instruments for looking at stars and planets.

Peninsula A piece of land that sticks out into the sea and is almost completely surrounded by water.

Vitamins A number of substances found in many foods. They help keep you healthy and free from disease. Vitamin C is one kind of vitamin.